THE

GHOSTLY TALES

OF

WINSTON-SALEM

Published by Arcadia Children's Books
A Division of Arcadia Publishing
Charleston, SC
www.arcadiapublishing.com

Spooky America is a trademark of Arcadia Publishing, Inc.

First published 2022

Manufactured in the United States

ISBN 978-1-4671-9871-4

Library of Congress Control Number: 2022932235

All images courtesy of Shutterstock.com.

Notice: The information in this book is true and complete to the best of our knowledge. It is offered without guarantee on the part of the author or Arcadia Publishing. The author and Arcadia Publishing disclaim all liability in connection with the use of this book.

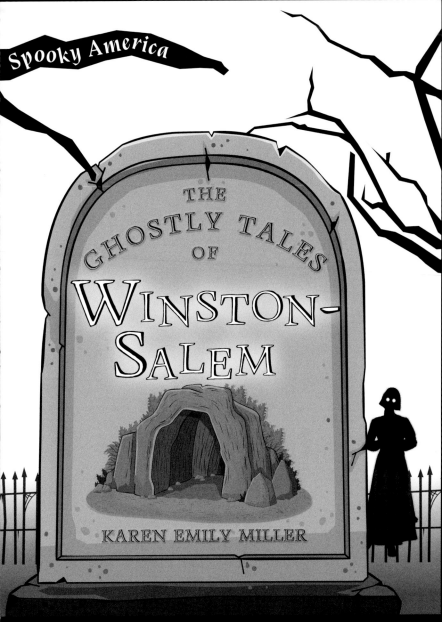

Spooky America

THE GHOSTLY TALES OF WINSTON-SALEM

KAREN EMILY MILLER

Adapted from *Haunted Winston-Salem* By Michael Bricker

arcadia
CHILDREN'S BOOKS

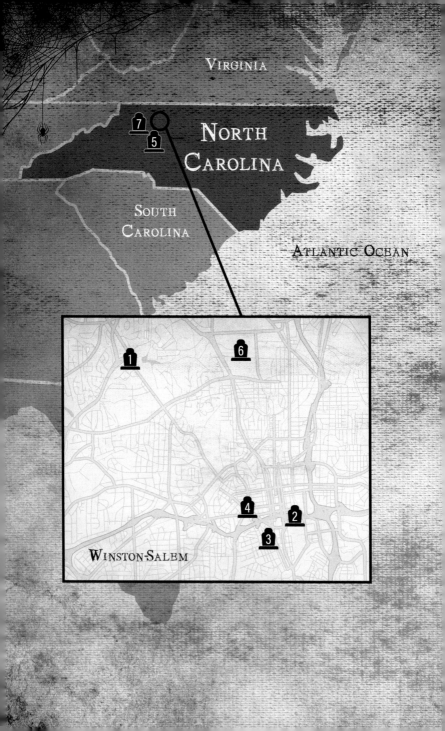

VIRGINIA

NORTH CAROLINA

SOUTH CAROLINA

ATLANTIC OCEAN

WINSTON-SALEM

TABLE OF CONTENTS & MAP KEY

Introduction 3

1 Chapter 1. Bigfoot in the South 7

2 Chapter 2. The Curse of the Earth 17

Chapter 3. He Wouldn't Tell a Lie, Would He? 27

Chapter 4. The Haunted Cavern 35

3 Chapter 5. Neighborly Haunts 41

4 Chapter 6. The Ghost Wagon 51

Chapter 7. The Haunted Grocery Store 57

Chapter 8. Are You Afraid of the Dark? 67

5 Chapter 9. The Cursed Painting .77

6 Chapter 10. The Last Game 87

7 Chapter 11. A Residual Haunting? 93

Conclusion 103

Introduction

The Cherokee knew the land around Winston Salem was good. They hunted wooly buffalo and deer and fished in the river. Their ancestors lived undisturbed on the land for over eight thousand years. They coexisted with creatures of all kinds, including bigfoot, some say.

The Moravians—German Protestants—came next. They thought the land was a peaceful haven, away from those who would punish them for their religion. They were brave people, afraid of nothing but the devil. That's why they didn't like the caves on the land. Some thought the devil might be skulking in one of the tunnels.

Winston Salem, to the naked eye, might look like a peaceful. However, if you dig further, peek into windows, and listen, you'll find it full of curses, witches, and ghosts.

So, when you visit (or if you are lucky enough to live in Winston-Salem), pay attention. Pause

by old wells and listen. Besides the trickle of water, will you hear the strange chants of Druid monks? If you rise before the sun on market days, will you see a horse and wagon that stopped running over a hundred years ago? Sit outside one of the old houses after the sun sets. You might see a little old lady peeking out the window at you. Enjoy the thrill, for none of those supernatural events could harm you. But if a blood red painting appears in your house, run! That's the one mystery of Winston-Salem no one wants to solve.

Bigfoot in the South

If someone says "Bigfoot," what do you picture? The hairy beast who roams the Pacific Northwest? Or maybe the ice-white creature who scales mountain peaks in Tibet? You'd not likely think that a hairy beast once roamed Winston-Salem, North Carolina. That's because you haven't heard the story told by the first pioneers.

Local Saponi and Cherokee people in North Carolina have many tales passed from one generation to the other. One of the stories is about Bigfoot. According to those who settled here, Bigfoot is not the evil monster you read about. He is huge. He does stink, but his mission is not to hurt you. It's to protect you.

Imagine yourself as an early settler. Picture yourself on a forest trail with an old man—a trapper. He was one of the first settlers to arrive in this area and is known for his wisdom and skill in hunting. Your family has just arrived after traveling for weeks by wagon train. Your

family needs food. You're thrilled to be invited along for a hunt. It's your first.

Every turn in the trail is exciting but scary. The woods are deep and dark and full of rustles, screeches, and growls. Sometimes you spy a hawk circling in the sky. A pheasant, so close you could have touched him, swooshes up out of the brush, making you jump. After a while, you relax. Your footsteps slow to the forest rhythm, and you feel yourself become one with the woods.

Suddenly, a smell seeps through the crisp autumn air. Earthy and strong, it jolts your

senses. It smells like someone who has just rolled in manure—maybe even eaten some, too! Then, you see him. At least eight feet tall, he's covered with dark fur and has the biggest feet you've ever seen. Something about him makes you think of a man, perhaps because he walks like one. But you've never seen a human like this before. Behind him walk three more

beasts: a female and two younger males. The female is seven feet tall. One of the males looks like he is six feet tall, the other about four feet.

It feels like someone stole your breath away or maybe punched you in the stomach. What are these creatures?

You wouldn't have a chance against them. Will they eat you? Their muscles ripple as they walked toward you. It looks like any one of them could rip a tree up by its roots.

You look to the trapper. Why isn't he raising his fowler gun to shoot them? A load of buckshot would stop them.

The old man holds his finger to his mouth. He whispers, "Look straight ahead. Pretend you don't see them."

How can you pretend they aren't there? You've never seen anything like them. Besides, you are certain they have seen you. You almost shriek as they make a move. But you clamp your lips together and follow in the steps of the trapper.

Then they do something shocking. Without glancing at you or the trapper, the big male steps off to the right side of the path. When the old man passes the large male, he respectfully nods his head.

One by one, the female and two smaller males follow. As they pass, you wish you could hold your nose. Besides the manure smell, they give off the scent of an outhouse.

The beasts keep walking, looking straight ahead. Finally, the trapper says, "You can look up now. They've disappeared into the woods."

"What were they?" you murmur, not certain if you can talk in a normal tone. The beasts might hear.

He tells you to hush again. This time, it's because he spots a deer in the distance. It's only after you two head back home, deer slung over his shoulders, that he explains.

As well as you can remember, this is what he says: "My Cherokee friends told me I would see the holy ones someday. I'm glad I remembered how to greet them. They have been here longer

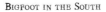

than any of us. Some say they have been here for thousands of years."

He stops and rearranges the deer on his shoulders. "These creatures are here to take care of us. That's why we must always show them respect. Besides," he says looking at you sternly, "If you harm one, your people will be cursed.

Years have passed, and the hunting trails have been paved over with roads and shopping centers. Much of the forest has disappeared. Yet, as late as the 1970s, there's been evidence

of Bigfoot visits in this area. It was around this time that a surprise snowstorm covered Winston-Salem. When people looked out their windows, they saw large human-like footprints. The footprints measured the size of a man's twenty-plus size shoe. That's more than fourteen inches long! The trail continued until the woods, where they disappeared.

A prank? Someone with a homemade mold could have made the prints. However, five-foot-tall chain-link fences separated the yards. There was no break in the stride of the footprints. It was as if a creature over eight feet tall had easily jumped the fences.

And there are still those who claim that they have heard Bigfoot. They say they hear howls and whoops in the woods. Maybe you could explore the woods around Winston-Salem and see for yourself. If you hear a whoop or a howl, don't be afraid. Perhaps Bigfoot is just saying hello.

The Curse of the Earth

The people of Winston-Salem knew about shamans, and what they knew frightened them. The nearby Cherokee put great faith into these men, who were considered the spiritual leaders for their villages. If there were a drought, disease, or war, the shaman was expected to talk with the spirits and solve the trouble. Communicate with spirits? To the Moravians, who had settled in Salem, this was wrong.

They believed that their god was the only one. Shamans engaged in trance dances to talk to the spirits. The Moravians did not think good Protestant people should dance.

So, when Running Fox, a Cherokee shaman, walked into Salem one day in the 1830s, the townspeople kept their distance. He explained that he was there only because his vision commanded him to do so. In his dream, he saw an evil presence near the town. He had come to banish it.

Running Fox described the land in his dream, and the townspeople recognized he was describing the Fansler farm. Perhaps against their better judgement, they showed him the way.

What had happened to the Fansler's? Running Fox did not know, but sensed that this was the family he was fated to help.

Farmer Fansler did not greet him any more kindly than the townspeople had. "What problems have you brought?" he is rumored to have said.

Supposedly, Running Fox answered, "I do not bring problems. I bring answers."

Something about Running Fox—perhaps it was his clear eyes or his look of concern—convinced Fansler he was there to help.

Farmer Fansler told Running Fox the story of his troubles. During the winter, a hungry family, the Jacobs, had shown up on his doorstep. They were shivering, without the supplies they'd need to survive the cold. Fansler was not a cruel man. He agreed they could stay the winter if they helped out on the farm.

As the long winter nights passed, bits and pieces of the Jacobs' family story surfaced. A Moravian family had befriended them soon after they arrived in America from Germany. They convinced the Jacobs to travel to North Carolina, where they could start a new life. The Jacobs family eagerly accepted.

However, that was the end of their good fortune. The Jacobs and the Moravian family became separated from the wagon train and were attacked by a band of thieves.

The highwaymen allowed the Moravian family to escape after they took their valuables. But for some reason, wouldn't let the Jacobs go. Even though they eagerly gave up their treasures, the leader of the thieves took against them. It was as if he went insane.

"You are sheltering a demon," he said, laughing hysterically. "And you have passed it onto me!" He cursed and screamed at the family, dancing wildly around them. Suddenly, he fell to the ground. He was dead.

The other robbers, white-faced and trembling, gave the Jacobs back their valuables. "Leave! Leave now!" They said, "Before you visit the demon on one of us."

After wandering for a few days, the Jacobs' found another wagon train that took them as far as Salem.

They thought they found a safe haven when Farmer Fansler took them in. But it was not to be. The winter was a hard one, and one by one, the entire family died.

Fansler buried them in a graveyard close by. He thought their bad luck had died with them. He was wrong. Somehow, the evil curse seeped into the ground in which they were buried. Soon bad luck, accidents, and illnesses beset not only the Fansler family, but also their servants.

It was then, that summer afternoon, that Running Fox arrived at the farm.

Running Fox nodded when he heard the

story. He knew he was needed here. As he had approached the farm, a cold, icy wind wrapped around him. The cold was sharp, almost painful, when he passed the graveyard where the Jacobs had been buried. So this was where the evil resided. Something had to be done—and soon.

He asked Farmer Fansler for a hut or shed. He needed to prepare himself for battle by purifying himself. He sat in the shed, made into a sweat lodge, for two days. On the third day, he stood on the threshold of the lodge and proclaimed he was ready. He directed all the Fanslers and the servants to accompany him to the graveyard. Terrified but anxious to get rid of the demon, they obeyed.

With everyone gathered around, Running Fox began the slow, repetitive dance of the shaman, secret moves passed down through generations of medicine men. He sang the chants to force away the spirits. People say the earth trembled, and gravestones tumbled to the ground. The five graves containing the remains of the Jacobs family sank into the earth. Not a trace of the burials remained. Trees surrounding the graveyard rocked back and forth. Their branches took on the shape of beasts. Moans, cries, and shrieks exploded from the earth where the Jacobs family had been buried.

Running Fox stilled. He stood straight and tall.

There was silence. The wind subsided, and trees stopped swaying. The branches regained their natural shape, and the dark clouds that had covered the farm blew away. The moon, full and bright, bathed them with its shine.

Running Fox left the next day. His work was done.

Nothing more is known of him. But it's said the farm, and all who lived on it, prospered. The Fansler farm was rid, for good, of the curse.

He Wouldn't Tell a Lie, Would He?

George Washington was famous for many things, some of which were true. True, he led the fight to free America from England. True, he was the first president of the United States. But some other stories about him may not be true. For example, some say he chopped down his father's favorite cherry tree when he was a child.

In those days, parents were very strict. He knew that telling the truth might get him in big trouble. But he was brave and admitted what he had done. For many, this story is an example of Washington's truthfulness. "George Washington never told a lie" is one of the best-known story about our first president. So, if George Washington said a cave was haunted, would you believe him? This is a story you'll have to hear to believe.

After he was elected president, Washington wanted to explore his new country. By visiting the former colonies in New England, the Middle States, and the South, he could learn about his new citizens and how to help them and the country succeed.

He arrived at the Paper Settlement of West Salem. The Moravian community there knew how to harness river water so it could be shared by people in the town. They used horses to operate the pumps and bored out logs as pipes. This was a skill needed for a developing country. Washington was impressed.

It should have been an uneventful visit. The settlement, however, was near the Witch's Triangle. Three sisters were said to live in one of the nearby caverns. The Moravians thought that such ancient, deep, dark caves must hold something evil. Anyone who lived in such a place must be wicked, too. The three sisters had earned a reputation for healing. People with heart and body aches visited the three, hoping for cures. Others said the three sisters did more than heal. They thought they put curses and hexes on people, too. A local teacher named Brother Steiner was George Washington's guide when he visited the Paper Settlement. But he was nervous about riding past the Witches' Triangle.

Picture yourself along for the ride. Even though you are riding a steady horse, you worry about the potholes and washouts from rains. The way to the caves—not a road but a trail—snakes through ravines and gullies. You

lean over on your saddle and look down. It doesn't look too dangerous. You see green, though there is no forest there. What you see are the tops of trees. If you fall, you will fall a long way. Perhaps the branches will break your fall, perhaps not.

When you pull up to the caves' mouth, you breathe a sigh of relief. But wait. Don't relax yet.

The president is curious about the witches. He wants to see for himself.

You step into the cave entrance. Its heavy with wet and smells musty, like Grandma's basement. From far away there's a *drip drip* of water. There's a rustle nearby, making you jump. It's too much. You run out of the cave.

You wait and wait. Was it minutes or hours before the president and his two friends disappeared at the entrance? It seems like hours.

Finally, they come out. You're just relieved they seem fine. Perhaps that is saying too much. Ashen-faced and grim, the president and his friends silently mount their horses. Not as word is said on the way to the Paper Settlement.

Finally, Brother Steiner asks what happened in the cave. Had he seen the witches? A glimpse of the devil?

"This is not my first encounter with supernatural and unholy beings," the president supposedly said. "However, I hope it will be my last."

What had the president seen? No one knows for sure. However, a strange tale about the cave circulated around Salem a few days later. Curious, a few men made the trip to the caves themselves. They explored the cave the president had seen and were shocked by what they saw. There were nothing but ashes, three piles of them. Whoever or whatever had been hiding in the caves was gone, never to be seen again.

The Haunted Cavern

Druids. Aren't they the ancient people who worshipped nature, wore long hooded robes, and built Stonehenge? Why are they included in ghost stories of Winston Salem?

It's said that once Druids were part of Winston-Salem history. According to the old timers, they arrived over two hundred years ago and settled in the caves of West Salem. Locals called them the chanting monks because of the songs they sang in their nature worship. People in the town knew where they lived, but the chanting monks very much kept to themselves.

In the early days of the city, settlers dug tunnels to connect to underground streams so they could have fresh water. But if you believe some of the old stories, these wells also provided a supernatural way to communicate with the dead. According to the stories, if you called down into a well, the departed could hear you. It made sense in a supernatural way. Both the streams and the dead were underground.

There was something else underground, too. Gold! During the Gold Rush in the early 1800s, many sought their fortunes in the caves and man-made tunnels in West Salem. These were good places to look for gold. But while they were looking for gold, the miners heard eerie sounds below ground. They claimed they could hear gentle, harmonious chanting underground. They believed that they were listening to the Druids chanting.

The townspeople grew used to the chorus of chants and were happy they had come to settle in Salem. That changed, though.

After some time, the voices became jarring, harsh. They told the listeners that their neighbors and friends had lied and cheated. Fights and arguments broke out among the settlers.

Something had to be done. The town went to miners for help. They knew every tunnel and turn below ground.

Would you have been brave enough to join the band to track the Druids? Picture yourself inching and stumbling your way deep into the earth. You only have a sputtering lantern for light. You hope

you don't stumble into a underground pool or injure yourself by bumping into a stalactite. Finally, after hours of crouching under low cave ceilings, you find yourself in a cavern so big that your lantern can't illuminate the entire cave. It's damp, it's cold, and you wish you were back at home. But you came here to do a job: find the Druids and stop the chanting.

The Druids, however, are nowhere to be seen. What you do find, though, is more frightening than robed monks hiding in the shadows. The walls are covered with strange symbols and primitive pictures of creatures.

The Druids had disappeared, but what

was left behind was certainly evil. All of you agree to destroy the cavern so no one else can see this.

There are many ways a miner can make a cavern disappear. No one knows exactly how they did it. But everyone agrees that once the cavern was demolished, not a one looked back.

Neighborly Haunts

If you were to look for a haunted house, wouldn't you start by looking on a desolate hill far outside town? Maybe you'd follow a rutted road into woods. You'd hope the path would lead you to a half-collapsed mansion.

If you're in Winston-Salem, you don't have to leave town. There are plenty of haunted houses right here. Start with the houses at 610 and 608 South Poplar—they are easy to find because they are next door to each other!

Let's start at the older of the two houses, 608 Poplar, which was built in 1850 for Mr. Reich. He was a second-generation shoemaker, respected by all. He worked tirelessly making and mending shoes. He did it so well that ten years after he started his business, he built a little shop behind his house. You can imagine him in his shop, working into the night. On a table nearby sit different kinds of leather. They're different sizes and thicknesses. You don't make all shoes the same way. Some need to be heavier, some lighter. Mr. Reich knew that and made sure he choose the right leather for the shoe's purpose. He would tap the heel on the shoe with his hammer. *Tap tap tap.*

Tap tap tap. That's how the next owner of 608 South Poplar determined who was causing mischief in her frame shop. Mr. Reich had dies, and Bobbie Ruff's family brought his house and shop. She was no shoemaker, but she loved to *tap tap tap* frames together. Once again, the shop was filled with the sounds of a hammer. Was it the taps that brought back the shoemaker? Eventually, Bobbie Ruff thought it did.

It began one morning when Bobbie found her framing tools and supplies scattered.

What was the mallet doing under the sink? Why were the tiny nails in a pile under the table? At first, she thought it was a prankster who had broken into the shop. But after a time, she changed her mind. Why weren't there any footprints outside? Had she heard tapping in the shop just before she opened the door?

One day, Bobbie lost her temper. She had been struggling to build a picture frame. It was already late for delivery, and every time she reached for a tool, she couldn't find it. It was when she was tapping in a piece of frame that didn't fit that she realized what had happened. The mysterious tapping and the missing tools could be explained. It had to be the shoemaker who had once worked there. What if Mr. Reich didn't like her framing in his shoemaking shop?

But enough was enough. He was gone. She wasn't. It was her shop now.

She straightened up and pounded her fist on the table. "Mr. Reich, I know you're here. I'm late on my project and won't be able to finish if you don't show me where the missing piece is."

Bobbie heard muffled movements in the back of the shop. "Mr. Reich, are you there?"

She heard a scuffle and a tiny screech. "Are you going to help me or not?" she called as she went to the table in the corner.

No shoemaker stood there. But the missing piece of frame was now on top of a pile of wood. "Thank you, Mr. Reich," she said. From then on, peace reigned in the shop. Maybe they formed a friendship. When Bobbie retired, she made sure she returned every once in a while. To visit Mr. Reich, of course.

It seems ghosts are part of the Ruff family. Bobbie's sister, Marilyn, also had a run in with ghosts. When she bought the house next to her sister's, did she know she'd get her own ghost, too?

Marilyn's family business was a flower shop. The original owner, Mrs. Grunert, had loved making flower arrangements. Like Mr. Reich, she'd work into the night, placing the buds and blossoms until they looked just right. When Marilyn took over the business, she put in long hours, too. She liked the quiet when the shop was closed to customers.

One night, she realized she wasn't the only one in the shop. A *scuffle, shuffle* came from the hallway behind her. Something was there and was coming closer. Marilyn froze, waiting for who knew what.

She squeezed her eyes shut. Maybe when she opened them, whatever was there would be gone. She was wrong.

A tiny lady—no more than five feet tall—peered around the corner. Marilyn studied the old woman carefully. Was she a customer? How had she gotten in the house?

She was small, but she was solid.

Marilyn gasped when she realized who it was. The late-night visitor was none other than the former owner, Mrs. Grunent, dead now for many years.

Had she stopped by to make sure Marilyn was arranging the flowers with as much care as she had done? For whatever reason Mrs.

Grunent stopped by, it seemed to be a good enough one for her to visit again. And she did, over and over again.

Marilyn's family and her customers saw Mrs. Grunent many times. Even passersby on the street spied her peeking out the windows.

Sadly, when Marilyn died, the 130-year-old business closed. Is that why no one saw Mrs. Grunent again? Since there weren't flowers or people to check on, did she say her final goodbye?

CHAPTER 6

The Ghost Wagon

Imagine an old-fashioned wagon, as big as the wagons that once traveled across the country, taking settlers west. This one is lighter and faster, though. It's the kind the farmers in Winston-Salem used when they took tobacco from their field to the market when tobacco was the biggest crop in North Carolina. Tobacco isn't grown as much here anymore. The farmers who do still grow tobacco use trucks.

But in the early 1900s, if you lived here, you could hear the creak, clatter, and squeaks of wagons rolling by your house almost every Saturday morning.

If you want to not only see but hear the wagon nowdays, you'll have to take the supernatural route. That's right. You might find yourself in the path of a ghost wagon.

First, you'll need to be on the route to farmer's market in Winston-Salem. Specifically, if you want to see or hear a ghost wagon, you might try positioning yourself at the intersection of Old Shallowford Road and

Broad Street. Secondly, you have to wait for a Saturday, which used to be market day. Finally, you have to be an early riser.

Farmers have to be ready to sell at first light. Many farmers grew tobacco, and they wanted to be the first to show their crop before it got too hot and it wilted!

You set your alarm for 6:15 a.m., even though the sun doesn't rise for an hour. You don't want to miss any farmers getting an early start. The clock *tick tocks*. Your eyes slide shut. It's too early to be up on a Saturday morning. Still, you wait.

Finally, you hear the creak of a wagon. You squint. Will it be hard to see?

There it is. The rising sun shines on the green sides of the wagon, lighting up the words "Nissen" painted on its side. The canvas top, rolled tightly over the wooden hoops, ripples just a bit, as a breeze passes by.

The driver wears the bib overalls usually worn by farmers and a wide-brimmed hat. Did he nod his head to you? Maybe it's your imagination. You watch him turning the corner. Just one more look, you say to yourself. Still in your pajamas, you run down the stairs and race to the corner. Panting, you shield your eyes from the sunrise and look. The farmer and wagon are gone. There's nothing to see but two rows of houses and the asphalt road shining in the morning sun.

Could this have been a "residual haunting?" That's what it's called when you see something that happened in the past. Maybe the farmer had an accident after you saw him. Thinking about it, you're happy you didn't see a tragic ending to his market day. You're relieved that your ghostly haunting showed only a farmer doing what he liked—delivering his goods to market. As ghosts go, the phantom farmer and his wagon are not so scary!

The Haunted
Grocery Store

We've seen spirits locked in place because they don't want leave their happy memories. What if a spirit gets stuck in a place because of a horrible one? That's what happened, people say, in a tiny grocery story in Winston-Salem.

The store stood on the top of a hill with open views of the city. A lovely place to shop, gossip with the owner Mrs. Tesh, and buy the best meat in town. Mr. Snow, the butcher, took pride in his work. If someone ordered a pot roast for Friday at 9:00 a.m., Mr. Snow made sure it was wrapped in paper, tied with string, and ready to go.

Mrs. Tesh valued Mr. Snow, but worried about him. He was an odd fellow, explaining his behavior by saying he had demons. He even claimed that one of fiends was Old Scratch, the devil himself.

When Mr. Snow was found dead one morning, Mrs. Tesh wondered if Old Scratch had won the battle.

The morning of his death began peacefully. Mrs. Tesh expected to find the daily meat orders wrapped and ready for delivery when she walked into the store. It was 6:00 a.m. and still dark. She heard the high-pitched buzz of the meatcutter from the back room.

"You can't cut meat in the dark, Mr. Snow," Mrs. Tesh remembered saying. She flicked on the store lights and opened the door. There, on the floor by the meat cutter, lay Mr. Snow. He was dead.

After Mrs. Tesh picked herself up off the floor, she ran. The police said Mr. Snow had an accident, but Mrs. Tesh didn't believe it. Something evil caused his death, she was certain. Her family cleared out every item on the grocery shelves. They closed the door behind them as they left. No one in Mrs. Tesh's family ever set foot in the store again.

The store didn't stay uninhabited, though. Weeks after Mr. Snow died, neighbors heard a racket of noises and saw lights going on and off. It was the middle of the night. What could be going on in the store? They called the police, but when the patrolmen arrived, they found nothing.

The neighbors on the other side of the store had their own horrors to face. Whenever the children went out to play, they said a monster came out of the store. At first, their mother ignored them. Monsters? Every kid saw monsters. It was nothing to worry about. One afternoon, though, the children ran into the house screaming. Between their sobs, they told their mother that the monster yelled at them. They couldn't understand

his words, but they sensed danger and evil in his bellowing calls. Could it have been Mr. Snow's ghost, their mother wondered? But when the children described a hulking beast, she knew it couldn't be Mr. Snow. That was enough. Buzzing shrieking, and mysterious lights were bad enough. But a monster? The family moved.

People thought the evil moved, too. But it stayed in the neighborhood. Some say said it took up residence in the newly empty house.

Moans and bursts of blinding light frightened the remaining neighbors. One day, the whole house shook and rolled, almost as if were in the middle of an earthquake. When the police came, they found shattered windows and cracks in the foundation. The house was so badly damaged, it had to be torn down.

Did that stop the evil energy? No, it moved back into the grocery store. Or that's what people thought. Flashes of lights and the buzzing noises got so bad that the neighbors on another side of the store moved, too.

All was quiet, for a while. A food co-op set up shop in the empty store. The first year passed uneventfully. A sigh of relief went through town. But then, one morning, cans and cartons seemed to shift and shimmy across the shelves. Workers would look for a missing item and find it aisles away from where they had put it. Even though the back room was locked, the sound of buzzing and rattling of the meat cutter came and went. The food co-op left as soon as it could gather up its supplies. Once again, the store was abandoned.

Stories fade, even scary ones. A construction company decided to use the building for storage. During the day, the only noise was made by the workers when they hefted piles of lumber and sheets of dry wall. At night, it changed. Even though the building had no power, lights clicked on and off. Still, the company kept the building open. As long as the sun shone and workers worked in pairs, nothing happened.

So, you might wonder, can you go and see the cursed store for yourself? No.

The store was located on the top of a hill that was also the perfect place for a baseball field. The store and the remaining neighborhood house were razed to make room for it.

If you go to the top of the hill, you won't hear the whirring noises of a meatcutter. The fluorescent lamps might buzz as they light the field, but that's all. You will see light, but it won't flick on and off. The only spectacle you'll see is a baseball game, not the end of Mr. Snow. That's what I'd rather see, wouldn't you?

CHAPTER 8

Are You Afraid of the Dark?

Are you afraid of the dark? No? How about an old, dark house? No again? You'd investigate, in the dark, in the old house. Of course, you'd take along your grandmother and her friend. That's because even though the house is old and dark, it's not empty. There's a spirit who lives there already. Put yourself in the place of a real kid from Winston-Salem who did a little ghost hunting in an old, abandoned house. Just imagine...

Your adventure begins one evening when you're visiting your grandmother. It's hot and humid, a typical Winston-Salem summer night. You and your grandmother are swinging back and forth on the porch swing, sipping lemonade, and waiting for the stars to come out.

Then grandmother plants her feet and pulls you up to stand with her.

"Look! The lights are back again!"

Across the street is a three-story Victorian, so big it covers the entire block.

"Grandmother, it's been empty for years, hasn't it?" You say. "There aren't any people living there."

You sit back down on the swing.

"Not living people," she says and points to a window on the first floor.

A hazy light fills the window and then disappears, only to glow again in another one. Your mouth hangs open as the light goes from window to window and then appears in the second and finally the third floor.

When you can finally speak, you ask grandmother if you can sleep over at her house the next night. The answer is yes, but she says

you have to help her entertain Mr. Elfred. Mr. Elfred's wife, dead now for years, had been one of grandmothers' friends. Mr. Elfred likes to talk about the happy days he had in the house

"It's his house," grandmother explains, "the one that has floating lights. I'm sure you'll want to meet him."

It's past suppertime when you tell Mr. Elfred that you have seen the lights.

Mr. Elfred pales, swallows, and says, "So, it's not just your grandmother who's seen them."

You both nod.

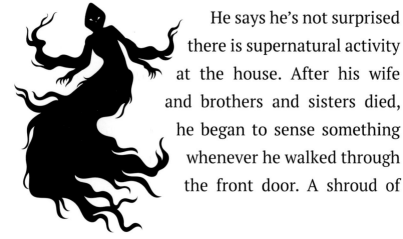

He says he's not surprised there is supernatural activity at the house. After his wife and brothers and sisters died, he began to sense something whenever he walked through the front door. A shroud of sadness, heavy and thick, always fell upon him. The feeling intensified every time he visited the house. Finally, he stopped going inside. He hasn't been inside the house for many years.

A blanket of cold, sadness, floating lights? Mr. Eldred has a ghost in his house, and you're going to help him get rid of it. It will be an exciting, scary adventure that would also be a good deed.

Mr. Eldred and your grandmother don't need convincing. As soon as they realize you are serious, they agree to a ghost hunt that night.

You don't have to wait long. At 9:30, you cross the street. After a check for vagrants, mischievous kids, you agree that no human is inside the house. At 10:00 p.m., the lights begin. A flicker appears in one of the second-story windows.

Mr. Eldred smiles. "I wonder if that's my wife. When we lived there, she had a ritual she did every night. She'd check every lock and window to make sure they were secure." He chuckles.

"She'd also make sure everyone was tucked safely in bed."

You run to a first-story window and wait for the light. You're afraid what you will see. You're afraid you won't see anything.

Then you gasp. A young woman in a white nightgown glides past you. She's carrying a

kerosene lamp and pauses in front of each window. The shadowy figure turns and smiles, but not at you. You wonder why she doesn't notice you. You're stranding inches away, separated by only a pane of glass.

Now you see why.

Two figures have burst into the room: Mr. Eldred and grandmother! They open their arms and call to her.

After a moment, the woman slides over to grandmother and folds her into a hug. You can see grandmother through the white fog of light. She's smiling, too, and with the shining glow surrounding her, steps up to Mr. Elfred. You see grandmother nod, as if she's heard the cloud speak. grandmother hugs Mr. Eldred gently.

By the time you join them, a warm comfortable light has filled the room.

No words are said. None need to be. You stand still, not wanting to break the spell. Finally, after some time, the aura becomes fainter and lighter. It disappears, and the room is once again, just an empty space in a dark old house.

Later, on the porch, you watch the house.

"That's the last time we'll see them," says grandmother.

Mr. Elfred nods. "She must have been lonely," he says.

"She was waiting for you to come home, one last time."

That was the end of our ghost adventure. Mr. Eldred wanted to make the house a home again, so he sold it to a young family.

It was the last time you see the lights. You hear laughter and disagreements and every happy noise that a family makes. The wife of Mr. Eldred has left to make room for another family, or maybe she stuck around to enjoy family life once more. If she has, she's making her nightly rounds without a lantern.

CHAPTER 9

The Cursed Painting

Let's imagine your family has lived in Winston-Salem since the first wagon trains arrived. The older generation knows every story about the old days. There's one that you aren't allowed to hear until you're twelve years old. It has scared your family for over one hundred years. You know it has something to do with the empty space over the fireplace mantel. Every time he comes into the library, your great uncle stops at the threshold and looks to the fireplace. He gives a sigh of relief and says, "Still empty, thank goodness." Today, he promises to tell you the whole story.

It begins in England in the 1550s. It was a difficult time. Crops failed. Family members got sick. People died, often at a young age. People had a hard time accepting their bad luck and tragedies. They had to find someone to blame. Often, they'd blame the poor, older women in their villages, those who had no one to protect them. These women, who sometimes made potions of herbs and plants, were accused of being witches. Sometimes monks or other religious figures were accused of witchcraft. In fact, it's said that an evil monk created the painting that was to haunt Winston-Salem hundreds of years.

How did this painting travel across the ocean to arrive in North Carolina? It's said that the evil monk feared for his life. If the witch finders saw the painting, they'd hang him as a witch. He had to hide it. So he gave it to a witch who had escaped her own hanging in England by sailing to America.

The painting was three by four feet in size. In the center, there were several terrifying figures. They seemed to be three-dimensional, almost as if they could leap off the canvas. You'd look at it from one angle and see a witch. Move an inch or two, and the witch morphed onto a cyclops or ogre. If you were to touch it, the canvas felt warm. It even throbbed if you could stand to hold your fingers there long enough. Those who saw it said it was alive. In fact, some said, at least some of the paint used in it was actually blood!

Not much is known about the witch who came to own this horrible painting. She was said to have joined a wagon train that headed to Salem. She left Salem not long after arriving and was never heard of again. But she left the painting behind. The cursed painting went missing until it showed up again in 1892.

At that time, the Zinzendorf hotel was the fanciest hotel in town, a fine example of Victorian architecture, and the pride of Winston-Salem. Townspeople hoped it would bring tourists to town and make Winston-Salem a resort city. It was a beautiful wooden building, as long as a football field and four stories high.

But there was something strange here. The monk's painting hung in the grand lobby! Those who saw it were shocked. The painting changed from day to day. Different people saw different things—ogres, cyclopes, and hags, for example. Still, people came again and again to look. Was the painting a curse if it brought people to the hotel? Yes, it was a curse.

On Thanksgiving Day, just six months after the hotel had been completed, fire raged throughout the building, burning the hotel to the ground in two hours. People reported that cyclones of fire whirled through the air. Nothing was left but ashes. Or so they say.

The hotel was rebuilt. Everyone was surprised when the painting reappeared! This time, it shared space with a painting of the German leader, the Kaiser. Again, it didn't stay for long.

America entered into World War I with Germany. It was not the time for portraits of our enemy. The hotel papered over the Kaiser but couldn't find the cursed painting. Gone again.

But not for long. It showed up several years later in a home. The owner had bought it at an auction, he said. No one knows why he did so. And then your family bought the house and its contents.

Your great uncle tells you what happened next. One night, when he was home alone, he heard voices coming from the painting. He approached it slowly, afraid to get too close. The picture changed as he moved closer. The witches and ogres and other monsters had become even more strange. Unable to help himself, he leaned in to hear the voices more clearly.

"We are coming for your family, tonight," the terrifying voices said.

He grabbed the poker from the fireplace. He stabbed and tore at the painting.

Nothing could harm it. After every tear or slash, the picture repaired itself. He said he could see the threads of canvas knitting themselves back together.

There was nothing to do but run. His family must be saved. He gathered them together and fled.

The next day, accompanied by friends and neighbors, he returned. As soon as they entered the home, they sensed something evil had happened. The painting and frame were missing. All that remained was the smell of burning flesh.

That's the end of the story. Or is it? Could your great uncle be afraid that he is still the owner of the haunted picture? Is it somewhere around Winston-Salem, waiting to make a return? Keep your eyes on that empty space over the mantel. If the painting ever reappears, you have to be ready to get rid of it right away!

The Last Game

In the early 1900s, semi-pro baseball teams sprang up all over America. Winston-Salem had several: The Waughtown Wild Cats, the Winston Blues, Salem Stars, and West Salem Red Socks. These local teams were good-natured rivals. But the Wild Cats stood out. In just a few years, they scored sixty wins and only three losses. The losses came only when the Wild Cats faced professional baseball teams.

Unfortunately, the league ended after 1917, when World War I began. Men were needed for the battlefield. Then, in 1918, the great flu epidemic took many lives. There simply weren't enough players for the games. The league ceased playing until 1920.

That spring, something happened to reignite baseball fever in Winston-Salem: Babe Ruth came to town.

His team, the New York Yankees came to play an exhibition game against the Brooklyn Dodgers on the old Winston-Salem fairgrounds. More than ten thousand fans came to see Babe. They came by horse, wagon, streetcar, foot, or if they were lucky, hitched a ride in one of the few cars in the state.

The field was makeshift, built over a horse racing track. No one cared.

Babe Ruth stepped to the plate in the sixth inning and hammered the ball over the infield to land on the track at the north end of the fairgrounds. It flew through the air six hundred feet and rolled fifty feet more.

That wasn't the only incredible thing fans saw that day.

Near the dugout, in the field where ball players and ball boys practiced, a different group of fans watched the game. People said it was a gang of boys they knew very well. Each of them had once been players in the semi-pro league. The difference between these boys and the rest of the fans was that these young men were all dead. They had either died from the flu or been killed in battle in the war. Fans rushed to the dugout, only to be told there was no one in dugout except for the men playing in the game. How could this be?

Most agreed that the answer to the mystery was this: the ghosts of the semi-pro players had come to see Babe Ruth. Who wouldn't?

That's not the end of the story. A few weeks later, new members of the semi-pro league passed by a ballfield that once been used by one of the old teams.

The ball field was brightly lit, which was strange since the field didn't have lights at that time. Everyone piled out of the pickups and Model Ts and ran to the field. There, two teams were in the midst of a game.

They heard:

"I got it!"

"There he goes!"

"Throw it home!"

Good-hearted jeers and jokes flew back and forth across the field. The men played with joy and grace. Sitting on benches were other players, waiting to be called in. Some chewed tobacco, spitting out brown streams that sometimes landed on the shoes of their neighbors. No one complained. All were watching the game intently, not wanting to miss a play.

Finally, they tore themselves away. It was late, and they had to get home. Besides, they could come back again to play, couldn't they?

But they never did. The ghosts of the semi-pro players had come together to play one last game. Can you imagine how you would have felt if you got to see it?

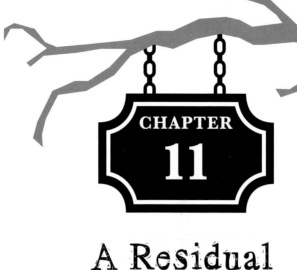

A Residual
Haunting?

Let's go back below ground. There are so many
old tunnels and caves under Winston-Salem,
it's not surprising that there's supernatural
activity here, too. These are ancient caves from
prehistoric times when the Uhwarrie mountain
range soared over twenty thousand feet. The
mountain range has weathered down to rolling
hills, but caves remain.

Then there are the man-made caves and tunnels, made when Salem became a gold town in the 1830s. Prospectors poured in and found copper and silver, too. Miners pickaxed and exploded into the earth.

This was dangerous work. A mine shaft could collapse and bury them. They might be trapped by a flash flood.

By the end of the Civil War, most gold, silver and copper mining stopped. But that didn't

stop people from looking for treasure. During the war, those with gold and silver often hid it in mine shafts and tunnels it to keep them safe. Unfortunately, they often forgot where it was buried. For years, scavengers, tunneled, dug, and searched for it for years.

That's why a group of workers found themselves reliving a mine collapse more than a hundred years after the Civil War ended. They were workers at RJ Reynolds Tobacco. Their bosses believed that there might be hidden caches of gold and silver in the basements of old factories. If there was anything that could be sold, the workers should bring it back.

The work crew from the Reynolds Tobacco company wasn't afraid. No one expected to find anything in the basement but old tobacco barrels. Those weren't worth much money.

They made their way to a factory basement. The smell of damp and the moisture in the air let them know they were near one of the local underground rivers.

It was hard to avoid the pools of stagnant water that had collected on the floor, especially in the dim light of their flashlights. They began to speed up, heaving old tobacco barrels aside as fast as they could. They were a little nervous.

Then everything stopped. Behind a cluster of barrels, there was a wooden door, over twelve feet high and twenty-four feet long. A giant padlock held the door shut.

More curious than frightened, the workers scrabbled in their toolboxes until one found a big metal cutter. *Rip, cut, snip*. After a few tries, they wrestled off the padlock.

What waited inside was a mine shaft so big, you could drive a large truck through it. That was odd but not too surprising. Heavy equipment for mining was often big. But why were the floor, walls, even the ceiling lined with handmade brick? The giant shaft had many smaller tunnels radiating out from both sides. What was this place?

The men decided to find out.

One by one, they ventured in. As they passed the smaller shafts, they saw lights twinkling in the darkness. Breath held, feet ready to run,

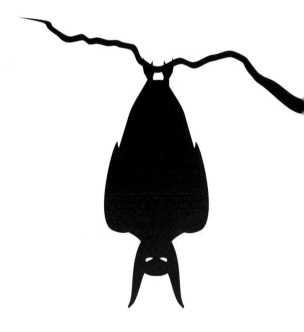

they inched their way in the dark. The tunnel turned this way and that, almost as if a snake had dug through the earth. Finally, after what seemed like endless turns, they found the source of the light. They saw miners, and they were working at a life-or-death speed.

The light from the old mining hats bounced back and forth from one end of the cavern to the other. The men could see that the miners' clothing, even though covered with mud and dirt, was the style of clothes worn over one hundred years ago. The workers were shocked! It looked like a scene from a movie.

But it wasn't a movie. They watched these figures, obviously trying to save other miners trapped in a collapse. Though they seemed to

be talking to each other, not a sound was heard. Their pickaxes made no noise as they struck the rocks. The workers called out to them. But the miners acted as if no one else was there.

They were ghosts, fated to relive again and again their failure to rescue their friends. The Reynolds factory workers turned and ran.

Later, they found out that in the 1830s, when gold, copper, and silver fever gripped the town, many men had died trying to find it. Although many were rescued, others were entombed in the caves.

Could what they saw have been a residual haunting? That's when terrible events, even though they may have happened long in the past, leave behind shadows of what had been. In this case, there weren't shadows—there were men, fated to live, over and over again, the night when they tried to save doomed miners.

No one should have to see this, the workers decided. It was too heartbreaking. They returned days later with a padlock that seemed

unbreakable. They promised each other that they would never reveal what lay behind the giant door. Some things are meant to be buried, for good.

Conclusion

Winston-Salem is a place of history and haunts. It's no wonder, for it's an old, old city. The town of Salem was founded more than twenty years before our colonies became the United States of America.

It's easy to slip back into the past here. You can walk in the imagined footsteps of the first settlers when you visit Old Salem Museums and Gardens. Some of the buildings there are restorations of the houses built over two hundred years ago. It's fun to imagine how people lived then. What is was like to read by candlelight, how to catch a muskrat, or churn butter?

If you like, you can even imagine what it was like to be spooked. Winston-Salem has an historical ghost tour in the West End of the city. You might have to squint to see the ghosts, for the tour is lit only by candlelight.

No matter what you see, or think you see, you will have an adventure!

Karen Emily Miller has been writing about strange creatures since she was six, so writing about the paranormal is a perfect fit. She just moved to Iowa City and is excited to meet those ghosts.

Check out some of the other Spooky America titles available now!

Spooky America was adapted from the creeptastic Haunted America series for adults. Haunted America explores historical haunts in cities and regions across America. Each book chronicles both the widely known and less-familiar history behind local ghosts and other unexplained mysteries. Here's more from *Haunted Winston-Salem* author Michael L. Bricker: